BLINDFOLD

The Hugh MacLennan Poetry Series

Editors: Tracy Ware and Allan Hepburn
Selection Committee: Mark Abley, Donald H. Akenson,
Philip Cercone, and Joan Harcourt

TITLES IN THE SERIES

BLINDFOLD

JOHN MIKHAIL ASFOUR

McGill-Queen's University Press
Montreal & Kingston · London · Ithaca

© McGill-Queen's University Press 2011
ISBN 978-0-7735-3847-4

Legal deposit first quarter 2011
Bibliothèque nationale du Québec

Printed in Canada on acid-free paper

McGill-Queen's University Press acknowledges the support of the
Canada Council for the Arts for our publishing program. We also
acknowledge the financial support of the Government of Canada
through the Canada Book Fund for our publishing activities.

Library and Archives Canada Cataloguing in Publication

Asfour, John, 1945–
   Blindfold / John Mikhail Asfour.

   ISBN 978-0-7735-3847-4

   I. Title.

PS8551.S36B55 2011   C811'.54   C2010-906442-9

This book was typeset by Interscript in 10/13 Minion.

To Jonathan and Mikaela with love

CONTENTS

BLINDFOLD

For the eyes, they bring us nothing.
I have a hundred worlds to create and
I am only losing one of them.
James Joyce

This growing dark is slow and brings no pain,
it flows along an easy slope
and is akin to eternity.
Jorge Luis Borges

A DIFFERENT WORLD

There's no joy
in losing
one of your senses,
it is a falsehood
that other senses will make up for the loss.

One fifth of the world
shifts,
turns into images
and the sight you once had
is replaced by a metaphor.

The vision you scanned the world with
moves
to settle in the recesses
of your memory,
to form permanent scenes
imprinted in your visual field,
etched in sharp clarity
like the pain of love
like nothing
other senses can be
a surrogate for.

Some retains its original value but the rest
fades over the years
or alters
into reconstructed pictures

caused by sound
and touch or
relayed by taste or smell.
Each sense

is responsible
for one definition of your life
and each question others ask
confirms your doubt
    something is missing in the equation,
    something you will have to do without
demands an explanation of how it feels to lose
something so valuable, so essential

to your life.
How can any of us accept
or, at least, understand
that it is only
the visible world being turned inward
or the world of sight and vision
transposed into ideas and revisions?
How, then, can you get to a point
where the loss is a mere non-sense,
a thing, a momentary frustration
when you try to locate
something you dropped,
something you hear rolling away from you
or when you try to recall your parents' features?

Once the judgment is confirmed,
tasting a plum is a poem,

or touching her skin under the night thunder,
and the smell
of April brings you closer
to being alive.
That is how you discover that the relationship between you and
the universe
is a pure theory
waiting to make itself clear,
only to be abandoned.

MEDITERRANEAN EYES

I leave the house
for coffee and a muffin,
my feet count the outside stairs
that guide me to the sidewalk.
The skin on my face
measures the temperature as the exhaust
of a passing car assaults my nostrils.
My white cane,
being an extension of my arm, feels
its way between curbs and lawns,
denoting driveways and cracks, certain
to trail the middle of the sidewalk,
avoid lamp posts, street signs
and trees planted at random. The city

catches me around the corner in noises and smells,
I probe for the pole to press the traffic light button
distracted by the thought of
another button elsewhere
pressed with aggression
or indifference
levelling cities to the ground
and consuming the flesh of thousands of innocents.

I listen for the cars
to come to a complete halt before I venture
across the street. Years of practice
allow me to walk a straight line

in measured and calculated steps to pass the intersection.
How many years has it been

since a mobility instructor
gave me a cane and watched me walk alone;
no assistance, no arms to hold on to
and no waiting for someone to take me for a walk.
He taught me to deal with all possible obstacles, yet
my forehead still needed stitches
after skirmishes with trees and posts.
I had the city at the tip of my cane and the streets

were mine to roam and stroll,
trying to identify stores and sites by smell
or approximation. How else, in the absence of friends
and books, in the loss of country and sight would I
kill the long empty afternoons
and catalog poems inside my head.

Even here,
at the bus stop, I could
meet a pair of eyes or a naked face
fixed and held in a gaze unlike
a gaze exchanged in the haste of love.
I imagine others looking at me, assessing
my every move,
wondering how I find objects and places,
    is the sound of a truck different from a bus,
    do other noises interfere with my concentration
    or how do I locate the doors and steps of vehicles?

I hear a woman raging against
all the cigarette-infected teens, their tattoos,
their pierced ears and noses, their
outrageous clothes and manners.
She fumes at
how they function and the way they talk
and the loss of moral standards and insight.
She ends her sermon with a tap on my arm:
"You really are lucky,
you don't have to see any of this."
The inside of the bus

babbles with languages I had hoped
to learn or read, traveling languages
that landed here to live another economy
and exercise the right to vote every few years,
languages willing to tolerate self-exile
and hoping to gain security in the process.
Here it is, the life of the city

characterized by its inhabitants
moving at a frantic pace,
composed or anxious, level-headed or confused
speeding to reach a destination, to open the factories
and the stores, to make it to an appointment or
get to the office on time and at the end of the day
transcendent,
a headline boasting
achievements of the municipal officials and the vigor
of the growth and gains in the country.

The bus driver leaves me at the wrong intersection.
I stand at the corner and wait,
try to recover and familiarize myself with life
around me. The policeman
who helps me navigate the traffic wants to know
   the cause and length of my blindness; about
   the fine print of the contract I signed with fate,
   the degree of vision I have left, the dog
   who will help me see into the future,
   and the possibility of borrowing
   the eyes of a dead man to keep them alive. Still,
he does not leave me empty-handed,
he asks, "Wouldn't death have been better for you?"
Momentarily blinded

can I recover myself
in unruffled speculations,
and admitting that I have never been able to comprehend
the behavior and composition of the human spirit,
create a poem of
   contemptible spirits and benevolent spirits,
   broken spirits and joyous ones, spirits
   that manifest themselves in words and action,
   spirits that soar high in time of passion,
and spirits that forever anticipate death when
death is ever present?

I want to shout back:

I rise every day and measure myself
against the trees and stones outside

that have notches and scabs in them. I greet my neighbors
and know that each of them has a narrative to scoop,
each has practiced pain and dealt with its crevices. Once
I had a body beautiful as prose
and the glances of a stranger close to home.
Once I had eyes large and dark,
Mediterranean eyes,

inquiring and tenacious eyes.
Eyes forever observing and watchful, able to see far,

the eyes of a boy ready to scrutinize,
clutch and imprison the future
and still, behind these eyes,
years of revisions, a will to live and
time have managed to plant a pair of deep-set eyes
about to create a hundred worlds.

I walk to the coffee shop,
confident
that she will be there, waiting for me,
ready to walk over and greet me,
kiss my cheek and lead me to our familiar table.
I shall feel the steam emanating from my coffee cup
and inhale its aroma,
knowing well that she will never be mine despite
the memories we carved together, but,
glad to be with her for these moments,
making a heaven inside the poem.

THE BLIND SHEPHERD

It was as if he had a sensory map
inside his head, knew all the shortcuts
to the fields and the mountain top.

Of course, the guard dog helped keep the flock in line
and hearing the bell that always rang
on the neck of the first male goat, he was
certain that no harm would befall the animals.

He'd come to depend on his cane,
held it before him in familiar places,
moved it left and right in a steady pace as a blind man does
and was not sure who he was without it.

Spring was the easy season;
the new-born popped out everywhere,
stood up on their feet and went to their mothers' udders.
He'd stumble on them and each time would thank the gods
who had a direct hand in adding to his flock.
Every now and then,

the wolves
would attack, steal a kid,
but not before he or the guard dog
put up a great fight. Noontime

would bring the goats to a stream and bring him
to the shade of a tree.

He'd eat his lunch and try to recite the verses
he'd made earlier and tucked away
when he felt the sun on his unseeing face
and the goats and the gods and the dog
were his audience.

He made use of all the islands in the Mediterranean
and his hero toured all of them only to return
when the longing for home and his woman became unbearable.

She whispered pleading he not stay away so long;
she did not want silk or gold,
only his voice to fill the house,
wanted to watch him sip her coffee,
sample her bread and in the night
feel her throat under his lips.

CALL TO MIND

I try to imagine
what it is like not to be blind,
not to have to listen to the sound of traffic in order
    to cross the street
not to identify things by smell or touch,
not to carry a white cane,
    remove my dark glasses for good.

I am so used to being me now,
after acquiring blindness as a nationality
a change would be a real shock to my system
and a real kick in the teeth to all of those
who have known me and still make the mistake
of thinking that I can see.
I am happy being me,

sitting in my chair reading,
having ideas and images come to me
and the sound of jazz over the radio,
a low current of desire passing through me
and moving on, replaced by memories
    the touch of the faces and hands of my past.

Maybe the way to get over all of this
is to imagine that child years ago
chasing kites and girls in a small village,
always, daring fate and enduring the outcome,
born to the same circumstances,

changing countries early in life
and coming home every evening to read
or listen to the news with a measure of skepticism:
a man in his fifties
translating the obstacles he has had to surmount
still hoping to bring about changes to his world
wiping a tear for the absence of love
and another
for his parents in a graveyard
away from their parents.

Uncle Nima was blind
to the end of his life
and none recalled why.
He obscured his name like grace
and wore it embroidered with sin,
as he liked to confess.
Like a busy broom without the bristles
severed off an oak tree, his cane swept him
to rare possibilities
and at times, to the edge of a cliff:
"I am Moses," he would say.
"I changed a snake to a wand, made love
to women in the desert
and had no desire to haul down tablets."

Tap, tap, and tap he would go
through cobblestones, tap,
tap, and tap into a cloud, ready to count the pebbles,
measure distances between eternities
undisturbed if one was missing.
"We escorted him everywhere," Dad would say
"but, the physical world meant nothing
beyond his finger tips."
In the fields,
we heaved rocks on his back
to build orchards and graves. On the mountain,
he stretched barbed wires
to fence a barn and a part of the sky.

He delivered kids
and lambs with no compunction,
the smell of blood or afterbirth never daunted him.
Grandpa would chuckle as he recounted
how the donkey emptied her bladder
on Uncle Nima's Sunday suit, how
he jumped in the river to wash off the smell
and drew the sign of the cross three times
to chase away evil spirits.

Uncle Nima closed his eyes
to challenge the light night and day
and the smile lasted longer than usual on his face.
He knew women by their voices and steps
and the smell of kitchens was his compass in the village.
Ladies would confide in him, touch his sleeve
or stroke his arm as he delineated secrets
he fabricated and rehearsed
recipes he invented for lasting love, but
his bride ran away the night of the wedding
after someone whispered in her ear
what a horned-goat he was.
His head would sway independent of his body
as he sang in the backyard
or poked his ear to free the hair from the wax.

Uncle Nima's dreams were cities closed to the world
and his imagination was
the only familiar land to visit.
In his darkness, he was a prisoner
leaning from his window

waving to other prisoners in the parade ground.
He rebelled against the light and the light was
like discarded shirts and ties in his cupboard.
A procession of faces was carved into the bones of his face,
layers of tanned skin and experience
sheathed the empty eye-sockets
and tears sprang between the lids freely.
The lines on his forehead, the stubble on his jaw,
the thousands of bumps and bruises his body endured
and the twitch on the side of the mouth
    a lithograph of unmet needs.

Before the final darkness claimed him,
He'd stare into the sun,
admit the light into his eyelids.
His face would break into a secular smile
and whenever he thought that no one was looking
Uncle Nima
would pass his hand over the front of his pants
to caress the fabric as he would a rare snake.

TELLING HER STORIES

My children have only seen her
in the album, knitting needles
in hands, creating first,
then delivering, mitts, gloves, scarves and cushions
in different patterns. They've asked

about dates and places,
wondered what jobs she held
and "What books did she leave behind?" They hear

her stories each time
I take her out of the cold ground
and ask her to make me
cheese, vine leaves or tea:

Child in the war, she refused to eat
bread made of barley and corn
and impossible to chew;
almost bled to death
and still lost the first two born
and suffered from iron deficiency and diabetes.
She specialized in mending clothes
and made a profession out of stretching meals.
She marked her life with artistic silence
threading her experiences like a necklace
on the line of her family tree
and span a clear vision of the discrepancy
between joy and pain.

The god she knew was a simple god who let her
question his ways
and puzzle over his plans on earth,
and she would visit with him at the end of each day.

Each time my children opened the album
to retrieve their grandmother's face
I wonder
if my mother ever
    absolved her god
or demanded of him
    his tears,
a divine penance for a
    blind betrayal.

THE STRAW CHAIR

He bought it for me
from the gypsies who came to the village
one summer and pitched
their tents by the river.

For three days
I traced the patterns of the straw on the seat
the carving on the legs the figures
on the spokes. I wouldn't let

anyone touch or come close
I would sit and get off, only
to sit again

I told everyone,
"Look what my father bought me."

I made up stories and retold them
to anyone who would listen.
I chased the genies away
at will
summoned them
to be present
to grant wishes
to assemble kingdoms
and destroy them around my chair.

I invaded every house and brought down
every clothesline,
chased cats and teased dogs,
terrorized the girls next door
and came back to make sure
that no one moved the chair from its place.

I read my books in the chair, and colored the world
and drew pictures of
other chairs and planned
to open a furniture store one day.

Each time he asked me how I liked the chair, I shared
the joy in my father's eyes
until that day
I heard his sobs in the next room
making real
the bottomless explosion
    a cavity ripped in the sky,
        my sight dethroned.

UNCLE

He changed
his name
from Yusif to Joseph,
later to Joe
and insisted on airing
a different tie every day.
He moved from Park Extension
to Ville Saint Laurent
and finally settled
in Park Ex again.
But he had his eye on the wall that kept him
away from Mont Royal. He orated
about all the companies
he could have operated
and all the boardrooms he could have chaired
had it not been for the failure of
his three sons. And his son-in-law was always
a source of recrimination
boasting his military history
trying to lessen the impact of failure.
My uncle cooked
his own meals,
ironed his days
and polished his own shoes.
We found him
sprawled on the bathroom floor
his bitterness
three days ripened by eternity.

SILVER THREADS

He recalls
the absence of sound, the impossible silence
the disappearance of light.

He is only aware of
the movement of his
mother's hand inside
her purse, looking

for her handkerchief.
He recalls her
warning not to play
with unknown objects
the type that explode on impact. Later,

he lies in the dark remembering
how she pointed out
the silver threads of the morning light
just the day before
and he sparkles
with guilt.

WINGS

They will tell you,
the healers:

soon enough,
someone
will break into my skull,
install a computer chip
in my visual field,
turn my glasses into
a video camera,
retrieve eighty percent
of my vision.
Then I will be able
to remove the blindfold
and see
George Herbert's "Easter Wings"
and my children's eyes.

DECEMBER 25TH

To hear their laughter,
to feel their excitement,
to watch them run from room to room
setting gifts apart
and shredding the wrapping,
two small beings
driven by their desire
to make a language of their phrases.

I will not say more
lest I be accused of affectation.

God,
poems must come to you
the way their voices,
unadulterated and clear,
come to me.

THE INTRUDER

Your body
breaks in every day,
and claims a front seat
among images and ideas,
it shifts easily
into a priority, into a reason
filling the recesses of my brain.

It grades each sector, leaves a trace on every frontier
it hides within, away from the trivial,
separate and pristine creating a world of its own:
a constituent of occupation.

Your body
pops in for a respite,
demands attention and finding itself at home
speaks about the worlds it can shape.
It spins, it stretches, it rests inside my head:
a cloud against the sun,
an answer to every quandary. I welcome

this interruption,
this unexpected renewal,
I sign over full awareness
and my guest assumes the centre of attention.
There's a technique in this enterprise, an invitation
to surrender,
to relinquish all senses,

to hold and retain this sought after intruder,
to stop all else.

Hold me here, in you, in me,
in the world and the world has no one else
but a presence of your flesh
colonizing and claiming the land as its own.
Sink your body into me and let me house it,
let me keep it as a secret
a fire of words and phrases, a desire,
a poem almost done.

A SUNDAY IN JUNE

My father visits
on a Sunday in June
inspects the backyard and asks:
"What happened to the
apple tree?" He takes
a chair to the shade and we talk
politics and tomato plants. He puffs
on his cigarette and insists
on brewing the Turkish coffee himself.

My son
shuffles over to his side,
explains the keys on his Game Boy
and my daughter invites him
to stroke her new cat.

He points out a few cracks
in the wall of the house
and before he leaves
touches my face wondering
why my hands have stopped
tracing the letters
on his gravestone.

BLINDFOLD

Blindfolded
eyelids fixed as in still-life,
the dust collects on the inside of my glasses
hiding the lines,
covering the watering of my eyes,
splitting the world of light
and I
aware of the restrictions

try to circumvent the world,
redefine its shapes and locations,
reduce it to an image
or to something I can touch,
something
within the reach of my hands.
I let my fingers crawl
along the sides of objects to gauge their nature
careful
not to tip them or spill their contents.

The quantum mechanics of sight,
there were other classical signs
all inside my head, of course,
beds unmade and sheets like wrinkled skin,
signs
easily explained
with some vision;

all the music, my words, my lyrical demonstration of what is
    possible
and the time I was touched on the arm
at the water fountain,
a silly game of "Who am I?"

I am filled with touch
and voice and sound
    voices and sounds
and seeing this mask
    their eyes make them deaf
    seeing only this mask
splitting my world
    for them what is away from my face
leaving what is inside my head
reduced to nothing, nothing but
images or the absence of images.

Is this just a veil before my face,
just a closing of the eyelids?
And will the light return once the eyelids are opened again?
Or
is it a momentary carelessness of some God
    distracted,
    biting his fingers, regretting an absence of mind,

leaving others to recreate me
    equating the man and the appearance, drawing
    associations between sight and mind,
their peripheral vision a blindfold.

THE CUTTING EDGE

Are we rehearsing or
is this the real performance?

Who is directing tonight,
I'd like to know.

Unreal, it is all so unreal:
The boots are wet, the mitts are lost,
the door handle of the car is missing.
This coat is too small and
where's my lunch box?
Has anyone seen the keys and who
left this knife on the table?

The faucet's still dripping,
the garbage is too full and
did you hear what the weather is going to be like?
There's an overdue bill here and who is playing
the lead this evening? None saw it happen:

the cat jumped
onto the counter and had her nose
in the salmon.

This part of the play
does not need a plot, it doesn't
even have to be included.

What do you think I should wear
to the theatre tonight?
Will there be any finger printing
and will anyone mention
the war during the intermission?

Please, let's keep this scene in for now.
If it doesn't work, I promise,
we'll take it out and go back
to the original script or
back a few years in the play
and let the characters rehearse
an earlier scene in their lives.

SURGERY

Remember the moon-shaped pillow
you brought to the office
and said I should use to support my neck
whenever I needed to lie down and rest?

"It would make it more like home,"
you exclaimed, we both smiled
and both your neck and mine
left an indentation on that pillow. Later in the day

the pain became intolerable
and surgery was the last option for the right eye.

Well, yesterday I came across it
as I rummaged in one of the boxes
in the basement looking for an essay I remember writing.
It looks smaller, the edges
are frayed and the moon
is less of a crescent than I thought,
the material has lost some of its texture and the whispers
we exchanged have vanished
to be awakened
only by touches or reminders.
Twenty years later,

I hold the pillow
in my hand and think about stealing
lost memories out of the past, reshaping

moon and material into something
less transient, less theoretical, mending
a drawer in the kitchen, a fence in the back
and a relationship tottering
under the weight of daily threats of war.

How can we build and break
what we built and where are the promises we made
and how similar is the war inside the poem to the world's wars?
A greater surgery is in the pipeline and
terms like pre-emptive strikes, collateral damage,
saving the world
and ridding the planet of weapons of mass destruction
seem nothing other than rhetoric,
and refurbishing a pillow seems less urgent
when the world
holds its breath
awaiting surgical strikes.

ULTIMATE

Death will come,
eventually,
to each of us.

When death catches me
on the sidewalk of a poem,
I will only regret
not having had you
   in my arms
long enough.

ANTICIPATION

Each dying day
I brood over
the bitterness of that last fight
and suspect
that quarrels are unavoidable.
No dishes were broken,
no screams heard
and the neighbors had no
stories to exaggerate. It was

a clear-cut refusal;
a certain tone in the voice,
an irrefutable "no."

As you left the bed,
I knew
that there was a death in this,
a termination of what was, a conclusion to history.
Our bodies would never meet again and I had to

turn the music off
and think of how not to presume
that what went on was predestined,
divined, predicted
and how in the end
we all become our own choices
and our bodies fail to remember what brought us together.

After this, how could
the heart be comforted,
calmed, assuaged, reassured or appeased?
The scene itself is,
no doubt,
common to any two
who have known each others' bodies

to the most inconsequential details.
What more is there to do but
dismiss the rejection or console,
begin again and revise, and can I, here,
subvert the text to get it right? Or to only say:
when will I learn
to acquaint myself with my consumed life,
with all the bereft days and nights
and how will I remove the implications
of hope and desire from it,
see it as a chain of events
that lead to what we all fear?
When will I learn that "no" is invoked every day
And this "no" was not
something we ever anticipated?

A SHOT IN THE PAPER

I can
imagine your faces
on the front page
of every newspaper
around the world. How time

stands still
and how all smiles
of children freeze
in a photograph.

But death comes too soon and
my unseeing eyes
fail to preserve you
in faded pictures
and my mind fails to understand
the motives of the assassin
who ended your lessons with a shot.

REFLECTIONS

Remove the blindfold
what do you see?
In a mirror
a face
two injured eyes
trying to calculate the changes
the accumulation of distorted kisses
under uneven sideburns
a mole
on the right side of the chin
some tiny scars that lead
to some other lines
that etched their way to the edge
of these eyes over the years.

I am a wild flower
on the highest peak of Mount Hermon;
I am the snow that fell over the years
to dome the rocks and prevent
the sun from stirring the earth;
I am the rain
that dropped one day
exploded
watering parched ground
and blasting flowers into light.

How can a detached retina lead to this?
The operation fail? The doctor

walk away? Into the snow?
Bring him back, let him reset
the stitches, steady his hand.
Thread the needle for a finer fix.
Shed more light to make him see
where sight is left, retrain his fingers,
place God in them,
connect what is lost with what is still living,
go deeper to the source of light.
Charge him to reflect,
reassess the power of his skills.

How can one survive this intense judgment,
How can one chronicle its delicate details?
It is only a moment in history, an expression
able to carve itself on a burning page
haunting poignant driven moment,
ready to be added to language and reinvent its shape.

Action surfaces in words
thrusting the text
into pure reflection.
And, if you attempt to erase the words
will they resist and nestle in speech
and if speech is erased,
where will it pitch itself, where will it seek cover?
In the mind or in the poem?

At thirteen, Grandpa said:
"Bring God to it if you have to,
shake his bones,

find out if his mistake was deliberate
or accidental.
Wake those slumbering angels up,
clip their wings or take their harps away.
This is not a day for songs
and the sin is not his
and he should not be in hospital
face covered with patches,
Band-Aids smothering his feverish frame,
and he should be in the fields
running after butterflies, flying kites
or chasing girls in the school yard.
And he should be riding the donkey
I brought him, training him for the harvest festival."

In the summer, the war travels from tree to tree
and we hide for a while under a branch
afraid that love will be taken away.
Ever since we've known love
there has been a war
and we've had no idea what would rise from the ground
or fall from the sky.
The planes would always come in waves
dip down and roar, dip down again,
plunge the earth and the skies into an inferno
and leave a million columns of smoke behind.
"I draw a soldier with a stick.
I draw a stick with a flower.
I draw a flower with a girl.
I draw a girl chasing the soldier away."
The hospital bed narrows

as your warm body slides under the sheets.
Your scent reaches me, settles in my mind.
Your skin melts the tips of my fingers.
You hold my face
your lips
finding their way around the blindfold.

"Let's see what you see,"
and he shines his light in my eyes.

I make a mistake
tell the resident doctor
that the blue light is yellow
and the red not so brilliant.
I fail to count the fingers before my face.
I hear the swish of his coat
as he moves away or is that a sigh
out of your lips?
I shall never know,

and I shall never know what it is in the poem
that clutches me and diverts me from the task at hand,
takes me away from the mirror
the reflection that does not reach me.
Something significant multiplies between the mirror
and meaning,
something whose nature I try harder
to analyze, to correlate
to redirect the theme
to feel a difference

between archetype and final judgment,
between what I am able to see
and the solid, cold surface of the glass.

What do I hope to find sitting here?
My younger self, my love for you,
The experience a man can't possibly retain?
The images of forty years past,
curled and tucked in a safe corner
of my mind? How do I reproduce all this
and how do I make it real or, at least,
turn the images into something tangible, something

I can touch, or taste, or draw on canvas were I able?
All the colors accumulated
in thirteen years, shades of blues and yellows, caravans
traveling south, carrying songs and tales,
bundles of history,
visions inside and outside my grasp,
horses racing to the end of the earth,
charging the land with hoof marks and neighs
and coming back with shades of light?
Or a faint pain, an imposed malformation of the heart?
The slopes of the mountain and lush gardens
or all the innocent secrets of childhood,
all the stories the neighbors learned to narrate? Tell me,

do they venerate the event yet? Do they
make a myth of the explosion, do their features
change when they recall the incident?

And do their eyes moisten when they retell that story
of a boy, just a boy
and his sky-filled eyes?

What blindfold can erase all this
become a barrier between the seeable and the seen?
How can love lose some of its glimmer

a whole world disappear from my vision
only to lodge its reflection inside my head? Let me

stop pretending that I see
the image the mirror sees,
the eyes that don't see me
and always reflect what I am,
always confirm
the visible permanent blindfold.

I shall be satisfied
to sit here
tracing what I can trace of my forehead,
counting what is left of the scars,
or trying to recall what caused each one of them,
being a part of the narrative and deciphering
its language which eludes me.
Gratified to hold the scissors
and trim the hair in my ears,
to lift my fingers and feel the stubble on my cheeks
growing ever so slowly
and needing to be attended to.

BOOTING THE PC

My children's voices after they
scamper to school,
the sounds and smells left
in the kitchen,
the cat looking for a soft place
to lay her dreams,
fragments of the morning news,
the weather and traffic jams
and all the wind and rain outside the window.

Last night,
the entire neighborhood gathered to decide
what we should do with the squirrel
after it fell from the tree
and bled to death on the sidewalk.

The love I sought in the night
was not there and will never be again.
Random visions of events
crowd my head,
form a net of ideas, intermingle
with words or impressions, a confusion
ready to be replaced with a movement
or an inclination to be the poem itself,
only a beginning, the lives of friends
lost to death or travel who will never be again
or someone standing at a bus stop,
buying cigarettes and telling a joke.

All this
before the desktop loads, before
the clock settles on the screen,
before I click on Outlook Express
anticipating your message.

CONFINED KISSES

When those kisses
were no longer spontaneous,
no longer stolen or
unexpected … near the kitchen sink
   or the staircase,
   on the way to the car
   or after a bath; as lips
   meet lips, touch, part,
   retrieve and start again;
   accompanied by a whiff of perfume
   from loose hair
   on shoulders or
   printed at the edge
   of a sleeveless dress

… when you turned away
I, unable to invite and renew kisses,
heard the note of my failure.

Kisses are confined now
to occasions; a birthday, an anniversary,
a something to hold on to,
scarce, barely
brushing the cheek, yet
   full of history, never
   to be repeated,
   never replenished
a breath expired

a spirit gone
a mind burnt. Leaving
our children at the edge
of a bridge
drawing their names on the water
blowing kisses, expecting
another boat to sail by.

DID NOT OWN UP

I wanted to tell you
as I caught up to you
on the corner,
as the light changed
and we ran
to catch the bus.
I should have said it then,
but people
crowded between us
and you would not have
heard me over the noise.
I also missed my chance
when we parted to our own work.
I could have told you later
on the phone.
Still, I waited till supper was up
when the kids kept us
both occupied.

In bed,
I finally had the courage
to say it
but feared disturbing your dreams.

BEYOND BELIEF

I still think
at times
that
I will be able to see one day
    surprise everyone I know
    spill the miracle on each corner
    race out to the street
and share my news with every passerby.

Tell everyone: I am the same man
with the white cane and dark glasses.
As I passed you by
you shook your head or labored to silence your
children's innocence.
I made you pause to think of ways
and means to approach me,
and you
took my arm to cross the street, asked me
the worth of living
sightless or
jumped out of my way to avoid collision.
I imagine myself
standing at the window
looking out to the street to see
what the neighbors are doing
    how far the paperboy will
    throw his burden.

Other times,
I think of trimming the hedge
pruning the tree in the front garden
waving to the woman next door
as she deposits her joy
onto the school bus.

Still, I think
of holding a book and turning the pages,
    pondering what to do with the printed page,
looking at pictures, driving
a car to the market

or throwing a ball in the park
for my son to catch. I think,

it is possible to live my life
without a cane and dark glasses,
without tripping over apologies, without drawing glances
when how I explore things or move
can be overlooked. Visiting far away cities
or walking among crowds,
unnoticed
is conceivable. A moment later,

I dismiss these thoughts and
inventing new romances
go to help my daughter
hear a lyric
in French.

IN THE METRO

They pass me by,
I hear their voices, their steps, smell
their perfume and at times,
I run into them head on. Apologies

ensue and I imagine
their jaws drop, their minds
race to make a comment,
or alter their reaction to rush
and offer assistance
instead of a damn.

Some jump out of my way
as my cane bruises their ankle.
Others ignore me and some
squeeze my arm
ready to lift me off the ground.

I am the darling of the metro riders,
my cane taps its way to the door,
finds an opening
and many jump to offer me a seat.
"Dear ladies, kind gentlemen, thank you.
This is humanity at its best," I'd say,
"this is humanity at the peak of refinement."
I can hear their brains humming:
I watch them watching me,
dark glasses prevent me

from seeing their eyes,
their urban clock
ticks away their own stress
and sidetracks them
from seeing beyond my external self.

I want to reassure them,
whisper in their ears
that this reality is less painful
than a pin prick on a cloudy day,
that the rest of what they see

is operational and we all learn to adjust,
that the blindfold between us
is only a thin film of moss
and none can envision what awaits all of us
at the next station.

On this wagon of the metro
we all endure the consequence of the night before
and bear the mishaps of our past.
We all speak to walls or to open doors,
to our cats or a glass of wine, to the emptiness
or the passion that gives meaning to the music
we listen to in time of joy or sadness,
and expect morning love will still be
love at night.

Let's find out before the next stop
how many loonies dance on a head of a pin,
how many ounces of democracy can we fit into one purse,

how many kisses can a lover tolerate before
his lips burn out
and how many deaths do we have to cause before we know
that our own skin is mortal? Let's partake
of all the secrets hidden in our pockets,
let's exchange sins before
the conductor tickets us for this assembly. A blind man

is a national treasure among you,
a symbol, a metaphor of all your idols
and you are such a great audience!
Let me then,
expound my theories, indulge me,
let me tell you what others failed to say:
the world we live in
is exactly what we made it to be. One day,
dear ladies, I shall
make love to you all
and gentlemen, I will preserve you
in a poem
precisely as you are.
Merci d'avoir voyagé
avec nous.
Bonne journée.

THE INTERVIEW

Everyone is impressed,
delighted
to meet me.
I have it all:
education, awards, experience and looks.

One interview after another
leads to the same rehearsal and drills.
The questions are direct,
the inquiries expected,
each member on the committee asks questions
about my specialty.
Some are more obvious than others,
some not so easy to discern.

I sit before them
formulate concise and intelligent responses for them.

They drill me, challenge my ideas.
No false assertion here, no priggish words;
we all agree that literature is the best of the humanities
and teaching is a noble profession.

I piece this together with no training in science,
these are my judges after all,
I need the job and they need my skills. They have
asked for the interview, haven't they?
They must have seen something significant in my letter
of application or in my curriculum vitae.

I explain the process of scanning papers and books
and the power of employing a screen-reader software
to link me to the world.

Then,
silence.
I hear the woodworms outside laboring
inside a tree trunk,
someone shuffles a paper,
I feel the stars shift in their orbits,
all the economical equations are rendered useless,
all the political theories are obsolete,
I wait,
love to make them squirm, love to
make them look for adequate
phrases and codes of behavior.

Then again,
I'd like to make it easy for them, like to
tell them what is politically correct
under the circumstances.
I know what they want to ask,
I know what they dare not ask, I know
and they know and I think,
why doesn't anyone inquire:

Doctor Asfour,
why should we take a risk
on a blind man?

THE CURTAIN'S DOWN

People surfaced as voices
far different from their features and statures:
uncertain, quivering,
sympathetic, regretful, shocked
once they recognized his blindness
whispering, intimate at times
and at times out loud, thinking
that if he couldn't see
he wouldn't be able to hear either.

Voices that would hesitate
before formulating a question
or uttering a statement
with a touch on the arm
or a tap on the shoulder,

voices that sank into silence
or challenged him,
teased and annoyed
and disconcerted his companions:
"Do you know who I am?"
Voices that would address his friends
expecting them to relay messages to him,
his own intelligence and presence
never entering the equation
and he tried to estimate how high
or how far the voices were,
how the speaker's eyes glazed
when his own demonstrated no reaction. He wondered:

is there a smile in those eyes?
Do the lips convey the spoken words?

Touch my face.

He feels his fingers on fire
and her lips smooth.
His veins fill with blood
and every fiber, every tissue in his body
rushes to change location.
I do not wear any makeup.
Her hair slides into his hand
and her skin documents all the passion he has.

He made his life
into a book of hours;
into psalms
reinventing her features in his mind,
a commitment to memory;
into a prayer for a
real vision
    of just this one sight.

He clothed everyone
in outfits that matched his moods,
sealed their weight to the level of their voices.
He identified their sex
by the sound of their receding steps
or the scent that trailed them.

He'd game at guessing their features
And in the absence of sight
hidden
behind a curtain
the sun
couldn't penetrate
he'd see himself,
a child in a playpen
receptive to sounds and smells
and a world that always eluded him.

No one knew what to do
when all the operations failed.
His father sat up nights
enumerating the misfortunes of his family history
adding sins to his own
and shaking his fist at the moon or the clouds.
His mother wiped her eyes
on her apron or sleeve
and applied cold compresses
to remove the redness. His brother
led him to the bathroom and laughed when
he came out with an open fly.

His sister added rosaries to her collection.

"Doctors know nothing about eye treatment."
"Take him to the magic lady in the neighboring village,
she'll chase away the spirits."
"Take him to a shrine –
saints have a soft spot for children."

"Take him to the West –
they'll replace his eyes with new ones
and he won't feel it."

He collected all the bits of advice,
tossed them like marbles in his mind,
rolled them between heaven's will
and the dictates of earth.
He couldn't see how any interceding power
or offerings could change God's mind
if God wished him to see.

In the night,
he would talk to God, argue or plead,
put his hand out in the dark
to feel his presence
and go to sleep thinking that
morning would stripe his window
and light would flood his room again.
He would promise not to steal eggs,
be penitent and he wouldn't blaspheme
or touch himself.
In the tired lines of every sleepless night
he became a god,
roaming the heavens, dissecting the stars,
rubbing shoulders with every distant sun
and turning everything that was invisible
into a theory.

DIVISION OF LABOUR

We have divided the tasks
to see if love is more attainable.
Now we can
devote more time
   to which friends
   you'll keep to yourself
   or which bills
   you'll pay,
   who will cook what meal
   who will wipe
   the table and afterwards
   who will clean the dishes.

I still envy those
who think that love is
the division of labour
an obsession with a particular taste
reacts to difference
changes or basks
blooming at room temperature. How often
have we struck a definition
only to restructure our vision
or moved into my insolvent soul
to enumerate the sins of my omissions.

in these cadences
notes are indistinguishable
and the picture of what there was

has faded from neglect.
I tread through the remains of my disillusion,
careful not to hurt what you relinquish
    or your fate.
Do I dare
to venture inward?
I do not use
this room,
    (but keep some shelving free
    for conversations or revisions)
I've left the floorboards bare
and never sought to
hang pictures.
This side of my mind
holds leather books, well bound,
preserved;
I have made certain that
the pages will never yellow, remain
upheld, dusted, inscribed, lined in order
alphabetical, and even in their composition.

How then will we distinguish love from
everything that is so familiar, or
those things insignificant, in
this new book, the rules of our submission?
    (How can we uphold it and say
    of all emotions, love is
    least mortal?)
Let it be an idea then, a phrase
that I can entertain when nothing
else bemuses. Let me

take it out, now, and then again,
for just a look
or to probe its temptations
or let me break it into another creation
a set of blocks
scattered down
along these corridors,
a puzzle for our child's amusement.

I fell in love
with the teacher whose name
now gone
I crammed onto my notebook pages.
She was tall and slim, she had
a smile
like an image that opens inside the mind,
long black hair and she made boys my age
assemble
or disperse like ideas. In the school yard,

I quarreled with two girls
who twirled her character on their jump rope
into a parody. I did not dare to show anyone
the poem I wrote for her.

The women in my life
have had some of her looks or manners,
all tossed their hair into a poem and challenged
my ideas into familiarity or resignation.
But none had an effect on me in the same way,
none sustained the images and forced the words to endure
and survive years of travel and experience.
Or
is it the ardour of youth,
so difficult to erase,
that visits infrequently
to remind me of its near absence.

FALLING OUT

It starts with something one of us
says, with something unintended, a word. It starts

with a sound or a gesture, something
needing to be finished, something delayed.
It starts with a picture in the mind
incomplete or not yet formulated, it starts
with a broken door lock, or
a window latch screeching to be
repaired. It starts

when the dishes pile up in the kitchen sink
and when the rug is overdue to be vacuumed.

It starts when the kids can't keep quiet in the back seat
and when they are late to school or their music lesson.
It starts when the bills have to be paid
and working late does not pay off. It starts when friends

smoke at the table in restaurants
or make comments that can be misinterpreted.
It is something neither of us wants to do
or bear the guilt for starting.

It is a sound lost in other sounds, coming
from the walls,
from the water on the river's edge, all the throbbing
in the mind itching to be said.

It is a rumbling in the stomach or a lump
in the throat. It is
all those promises and mistakes,
all the hopes unfulfilled. It is
a hand-painted ball I broke
accidentally.
It is an article in the paper full of falsehood

justifying walls to come down
and cities to be occupied.
It is something you always feared as a child
while others turned it into an art. It is

the body breaking into islands and the mind
unable to recover in time.

BLACK HOLE

Do you
want
to know how
it feels
    to be blind?

How the original pain
invades the other senses
and turns into rage, an unusual frenzy
    as if from another language
or a fever of anticipation?

Do you want to know
how mistakes are made
when God
rests
in the afternoon; when he
turns his back and
innocent curiosity is twisted
into a nightmare or a sin
reluctant to be erased?
The child ties his shoelaces
runs into a multitude of colors, tears his clothes
on the neighbor's fence, he meets a bomb
and together, they ignite into darkness.

    Day after day, you wait
    for the light to return;

for shapes and forms to reappear
as you open your eyelids.
You wait for the blame to be assigned, for answers,
for a sign or an explanation.
You beg and plead and demand
of the prayers to do the job
to have the judgment reversed. You wait

for the world to right itself
and for the cosmos to show its face
as it did once before
on a clear summer night.
You do not anticipate that every move
will be a challenge
every breath a hope.

You wonder why the fates remain silent
and why the shrines you visit
do not reveal their miracles.

The man accepts what is real,
reinvents his curiosity
and looks for a cryptogram
to consecrate his new mystery.

Darkness around you has no boundaries
unless it is marked by a tree
or a lamp post that cuts into your forehead.
Walls materialize before your face
out of nowhere and in a snowstorm

landmarks disappear and nothing guides you
but the endless sounds of silence. You count

your steps
unable to pack into your luggage
all the stings of travel:
the uprooting of home, lovers ignoring you,
a child dead two days into the light,
years of unemployment and
a marriage breaking down,
the embarrassment
of spilling sauce on your tie
– unmindful of finitude

he stays here
in these rooms far too large
for his aging body. The place
wants nothing of him and tomorrow
he will see the limits of the dream
and will have to leave with the light.

Those earthquakes and the floods,
all the wars and in the wars,
all the bombs detonated indiscriminately,
grieving mothers and orphans,
souls moving on too early or too soon
invading God's silence
and confusing his original plans,
all accumulate and he wonders
if they are part of the mistake or an attempt

to rectify the errors. He, an artist,
keeps trying to find the right colors, the vividness,
the passion that would only redefine the darkness, disappointed
by his failure to organize
a more insightful world.

Those cities built on the edge
of the clouds, the castles
leaning on the shoulders of storms, all the windows
on the other side of the sun
all the stories and debates of loss
and the choices given and then
taken away, all fall
into the dark. After this,

    after the years of getting here
    you still believe in a God
    beyond the temporal limit, after
    you have your doubts, and when you
    understand all the accusations hurled at him,
    the loneliness he lives in when things go wrong,
    understand the light born out of darkness
    and the darkness that is "akin to eternity," you, too,

feel ensnared and
beguiled by the deepening stillness
like God, really,
blinded and trapped
in a black hole.

EGGS

All the kids in the neighborhood nipped them
raiding barns,
hiding in the alleys
waiting for the chickens to lay their passion
or for the farmers to wager their crops,
holding back for the first opportunity
to launch the attack
and come out with the prize. The keys

to the barn were always hidden under a doormat
or in a crack over the threshold:
enter, young thieves,
make sure not to alarm the rooster,
slide an egg into a pocket,
smooth the hay in the chicken coop,
hide all evidence of sin.

The world
was smaller then,
no borders to speak of,

no barbed wires to rip our clothes.
The sky was no ceiling and our walls
went on and on over the slopes of the mountain
and the names of far away cities
hatched bold specks in our atlas
or different colors in geography books
and did not include girls our own age.

We had no business robbing
someone else's property,
didn't have the right gear, no name tags
and no identity papers in our pockets.
We didn't even have the traditional bow and arrow
in case of combat.

Away from our covert expeditions,
the eggs came to us boiled at times
and at times fried

unsummoned for breakfast
or in colors or baskets at Easter.
Their shells,
their yellow and white
stood on the horizon a silhouette, an easy target
like roses, like songs
that traveled here seasons ago
and stayed.
Farmers turned a blind eye to our mischief,
the guards at the edge of town
did not fingerprint us,
the priest did not profile any as sinners
and the chickens did not care who snatched their eggs:
they gave them away or folded them
under their wings for forty days
and could not hide their joy
when the beaks of new chicks broke the shell.

The man who sat in the church yard
sweeping the sweat off his brow,

laboring
with the summer heat, sighed and opened
his ice box
    a mournful fence
    urging us to profit
    exchanging
two eggs for three ice creams.

MORNING COFFEE

I am going to listen
to the man
sitting across from me
holding his coffee in his left hand, sipping,
his lips crowding the handle and his words
surfing the rising steam. I am going

to listen,
I will be attentive, courteous
and deferential.
I will be mindful
of how many rooms he will rent, how
many beds he will buy and who will keep the kids.

I will not analyze, scrutinize
or probe, will not ask about his income,
his rent or the age of his car. I will not

think of any of my indiscretions
or discord, will not
voice any profanities,
refrain from telling jokes,
avoid discussing politics or literature.
I will not compare hernias
or ulcers
and will not once allude
to sex or the war in Iraq.

Chances are
that one of us
will not be here tomorrow.

OBLIVIOUS

He repeats words of love
to her,
goes over the happy days and
reminds her of how devoted he is.

He can't sleep, can't eat
can't live like this.
He can't keep the nightmares away
and has to deaden the pain with apprehended stress.

He is not able to work.

"Can't you see that I need you?" he says
at dinner. "Don't you know
that I can't live without you?"

She listens as he talks,
hands him a napkin to wipe his glasses.
He cannot believe that love can be stifling
and his passion can crowd her, reduce
and imprison her.
He talks about renewing the promises
and breaking all the patterns
which made staying together impossible.

Before the cake and coffee are served
he tells her he wants her at any cost.
She gathers her purse and as she walks out
he is oblivious to the scream
inside her head.

They showed me nothing.
I must have been twelve
and they, older,

as the story goes,
two older girls, I met
in the school yard.
I must have done something
to make them notice me
and they started teasing,
pointing at the traces of hair
on my upper lip,
then my sideburns.
Then they lowered their gaze
 and blushed or giggled,
I don't really remember.

They whispered to one another,
asked me to meet them later that day
behind the barn, one said
and the other tantalized,
"He needs permission,"
and "Do you think he can?"
The words hung in the air.

It was summer then
and all the days were identical,
full of sun and play.

I said, fine, I'd meet
them at dusk and bring no one,
just me and them.
And then, they did not show.

I still can see their dresses
ballooning as they ran away
and I sprinted to help the younger girl as she tripped.
They said they had to go home
to lunch or to fix their hair.

I never saw those girls again,
they moved away or went to work at a summer job.
That was a fine day

running along with two beautiful girls,
rounding the corner
or holding hands, even climbing to the roof of that barn
to find a hiding place.

Did I think then that
I'd be fifty-five
turning the key to my home in another country
remembering them,
imagining them,
those girls, hiding behind the wall of the barn
waiting for me or was it someone else,
adjusting their hair,
growing older?

PASSING DESIRES

To pray again with the same delight
away from all doubts,
to give reason and faith equal worth
with no scorn and no derision,

to live in a world
free of discord and acrimony,
and to tell each other, "there's no need
for war,
no need
for the logic of weapons."
All we need is a dream of
poverty eradicated and crime
terminated.

There would be no need for jails and all the judges
would have to retire
or turn their experiences into fiction.
Their heroes would be characters of the past,
their challenge
not to long for podiums
and the thrills of the courts.

Every tree, every blade of grass
every cloud
could live
and birds and animals migrate
back to their dwellings. The earth
would experience four seasons
and poems would not have to be rewritten.

REPUDIATION

We tossed love
into the wastepaper basket
along with the torn
bills, fliers, crumbled
letters and nail clippings.
We lie around munching
on the ends of novels, mind-numbing
articles in the paper and
toasted bread smeared
with peanut butter, waiting
for a modern angel
to materialize out of the Internet
or come down via satellite
to shake us
back into speech.

The few words we exchange
sound decomposed and mistaken.
Two people
watching a play in which
the bad guy and the good guy are
played by one actor
for no reason
other than added suspense
or an attempt to cut down on cost.
The sound of a lawnmower reaches us,
followed by the smell
of freshly cut grass

and screech of tires.
Something is happening outside us,
lacking in emotions and ideas, something
relevant to time and action elsewhere,
something that each of us
will interpret into different
rules, producing dissimilar results.
Tomorrow,
as we discover that we both travel
on the back of every mistake,

one of us will have to
empty the wastepaper basket
and discover the remains
of a discarded sleeping pill.

SECOND HAND LOVE

In the centre of this
incoherent arrangement,
    remnants of unspoken agreements,
    sounds of musical instruments,
nothing remains.

What is permanent
is a carpet frayed on the side
a sticker on the wall,
a piece of a foam nail you attached
to the leg of a chair
in order not to scratch the kitchen floor.

All the peripheries of things
and how we spent hours
trying to glue together
a broken hockey helmet
only to discard it in the end.

Fifteen years
and three before that
and we found out that time spares no one,
learned how to accept that love
has nothing to do with this,
    ah, but tolerance does
    and human closeness.

When love reaches us
we carry it
to the house and sleep
    with it
only to wake to the sound
of our lips forming words
familiar to any two people
who have shared meals together
or
argued about who was going
to wash the kitchen floor next.

Or simply
signed a bank document.

Where second hand love
reaches us
we hide behind formalities
and never let on
that explanations are needed
to make sense of what we feel,
    while others in our lives
    wonder, yet never speak.
And the sum of how we got here becomes
a disputed calculation of events
and regrettable phrases uttered
during miscellaneous disagreements.

These litanies
of our existence are
mere lines

in freshly opened letters
containing no news,
no invitation to something
we care to attend,
creating
insidious nets
of tales whose traits have defined
what we are.
We know, in simple,
how to avoid charges
and accusations that may level
this history of what we have built together. Out of courtesy
on occasions
you turn your cheek to me,
never your lips.

SHORT OF HISTORY

We need history in all of this,
need accumulated memories,
friends to gossip about
and stories to exaggerate. We need time

to walk the streets of the city
itemizing shop windows and ducking the traffic,
time to shelter in cafes,
read remnants of discarded newspapers
and solicit the waiter to fill our cups.

There's a certain politics we missed
in being on either end of the sidewalk
and a culture of acceptance to identify,

a dinner to cook together
and the smells of bread in a shared kitchen.

There's a need to go from one room
to the next looking for objects and misplaced items,
exchanging random words or phrases.
Why do I sit here, at the edge of the bed,
watching you apply your makeup,
adjust a strand of future,
press your lips
trying to catch what is left of life,
file it under your arm
and walk with it. Most of us

live inside our heads
and very little of what we feel or think is
in our speech.
We try to find joy in one incident or another
in what touches or moves us. We try
to bridge what we missed or reconstruct
the years into an agreeable present.
How I seek you
ready to change my reality, ready to be
a part of yours. All the books I love to read
are hidden in your eyes and I would
exchange a culture, amend a belief,
if I only could make this possible.

WAITING

Just past the sunrise
we all
stand in line,
waiting our turn to get a number,
to hold on
to a piece of paper that
will identify us. Each one is
assigned a task or a
share in a task. Some may

finish the assignment and some never.
But we all try. I, too,

spend my days looking
at my number,
wondering when I will be
called and when the darkness
will complete the day.

CASUAL HANDSHAKE

For Edward Said

Give me your pen and enter my mind,
take your place in a new exile,
and let us write of a handshake between us and countries
ready to be born.
Dictate your lines and fill the page,
whisper in my ear.
Tell me how the rebel dies and the poem remains real,
how the words inscribe a new lease to freedom, erect borders,
build a house and open a street,
raise a flag on each lawn
and enter the age from the Eastern gate. Give me your pen

and let your fingers rest.
Let me move my lips for you;
let me reroute all the contracts,

all the resolutions on the shelves of the UN
and draw a new map.
Place Jerusalem at center stage
and tell me how, in building a country, you stumbled upon death,
snubbed its vigour, slowed its march
and how you will live in the books and the minds; a sane vision,
a miracle, a passport, and shall we say

there's an eventual wedding on the horizon
and a bride sliding into her dress,

a country being born out of the rubble,
a people breaking all shackles
and obliterating prisons. Or shall we say

how you happened
into our lives and held assemblies of the mind
with Joyce, Conrad and Proust,
with Darwish and Maghut, how you and they
have walked into your exile
only to redefine what we write, a language,
only to build your own city.
How you erased all the lies hurled at you, at us
with no hint of any logical
or even narrative structure to support the offence.
How you removed the slander from our history,
wiped the slate clean and taught us
to be proud and turn each exile into a homeland,
taught us to seize on an image to proclaim
as long as our skin holds our bones.

Your chisels sharpened and oiled,
your words, alchemy
cutting through all the chatter,
you toured the world to unclutter our case,
to reinvent a concept for peace everywhere.
You trained each of us to count our desires
and not to fear passions of the mind and the body;

desires to cross borders without checkpoints,
to be free, not to be fingerprinted or profiled,
not to be defaced on any screen or front page,

desires to read and understand
and to walk into the sun human and informed.

When much of the light in the universe
has not yet reached us,
you leave and the tents still crowd the land,
the bombs pour down, houses are ripped from the earth,
and the olive trees are hacked and uprooted.
The flames in the East rage on and all the treaties
are deferred. The war dominates the whole century
and petitions everyone. The others die
and we die.

You leave and only the question remains:
has our suffering been less painful
and as they close their eyes,
have our dead been by all measures unlike theirs?

WE ONLY MEET IN A POEM NOW

For Louis Dudek

How do the features of the city change
and when is the present tense no longer applicable?
How did you pass into the damp ground
and leave poetry unattended?

You and I
drilled death, waged war on the poem
and never knew that it would create such a distance between us.
Everywhere you leave something, you leave no one,
leave the books and the music notes,
leave us unable to write. All the lampposts
are plastered with faded paper signs and the trees
on Ste-Catherine street are leafless.
There's no war here but a fabricated threat
of terrorism.
The criminal law is rewritten
and racial profiling is permissible.

Children are dying elsewhere
and their deaths do not reach us in time
to instigate more grief.
All the headlines in all the papers
have declared the loss of that familiar innocence
and we all have embraced a nightmare
unlike any our ancestors
lived through. The features of the city
have changed and we sold civil liberty

after you left.
Why am I so full of fear
unable to unearth you, fill you in
on how we get on in your absence?

Another Christmas has passed and you have missed
our rendezvous.
A lunch and a coffee and an exchange of gifts
that we both promised we wouldn't buy the year before.
Then, you bring out your notebook
and read to me:
"Our age is not the age of the poem,

and this country will never rise to our ideals,
nor will death change what we are."

Let me ask again:
where does the soul go
after we close our eyes
and where the memory of the languages?
And is the still body
the only fragment that remains?
Does the poem suffice when all else fails?

Your place in history has not been made
and one day, this country will have to transfer
your words and passion into action.
One day, we will all have to die
or be hypnotized by the smile
inside the words you left
by the power of death and by the power of your lines.

Let's assume, then, that the mind has it all
yet refuses to relate it in language
or sleeps
to protect what should never have been said or written.
How were you able to pour all of it out
and be elated by the experience.
How you alone knew the course of events
and the direction this country would choose?
When I stand,

here, close to the walls of the library,
it is not the books or the notes that come to me,
not the awards and recognition.
It is not death or music that haunts me,
not the fate of our planet or who will wage the next war:
it is your voice reading and assessing,
explaining and debating concepts and theories,
giving literature its power of renewing itself;
it is your passion to live and educate, your love of the poem,
exposing our greatness and making us vulnerable.

It is your warm smile.
But still, an old argument
rises to my lips:
    what is the worth of this
    country
    which does not return your passion?
    What is the meaning of a poem
    that cannot be heard?

ACKNOWLEDGMENTS

The author would like to thank the Conseil des Arts et des Lettres du Québec for their generous support.

Thanks to the Historic Joy Kogawa House, Vancouver, B.C., for choosing the writer to be the 2009 inaugural writer-in-residence where *Blindfold* was completed.

Thanks also go to the following:
Ann-Marie Metten, Christiane Hayward, Elee Kraljii Gardiner, Allan Hepburn, Tracy Ware, Madeleine, Rawi, Majdi, Georges, Rose, and Lucie.